Foreword

Guitar Rock Shop is a complete, stand-alone method for rock guitar that is correlated to *Belwin's 21st Century Guitar Method.* You will learn rock and blues riffs, power chords, lead scales, and classic rhythm and lead guitar patterns as played by the guitar greats.

As are all the books of *Belwin's 21st Century Guitar Library,* the *Guitar Rock Shop* series is designed to build musicianship, develop the ear, and encourage creativity by providing a carefully thought-out, musical, and fun way to learn. Everything is explained and demonstrated on the included play-along recordings.

- CONTENTS -

Cassette users: For easy location of all programs, always set your tape counter to 000 when beginning the tape. Fill in the index numbers as you progress through the recording.

A Very Special Thanks

...to my wife, Audrey, for her unswerving support,

...to Sandy Feldstein, without whose suggestions and guidance this book would not have been possible,

...to Richard Hoover of the Santa Cruz Guitar Company and Tom Anderson of Tom Anderson Guitars for the use of their amazing instruments.

This book is dedicated to my daughter, Kelsey Rae.

Editors: Sandy Feldstein & Aaron Stang
Cover Design: Frank Milone & Ken Rehm
Photography: Roberto Santos
Sound Recording and Sequencing: Ray Lyon

The Guitar
Electric

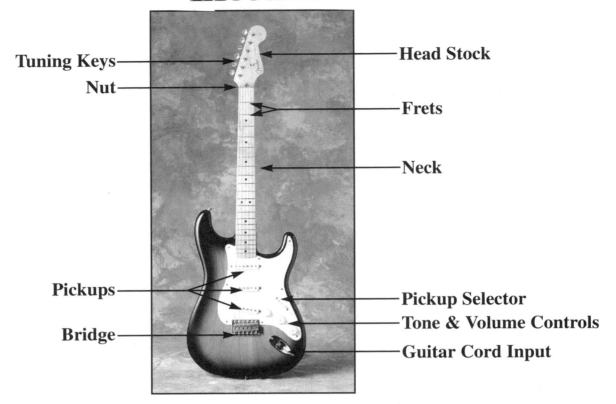

Tuning Keys —

Nut —

Pickups —

Bridge —

— Head Stock

— Frets

— Neck

— Pickup Selector

— Tone & Volume Controls

— Guitar Cord Input

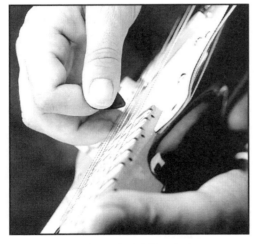

The pick should be held firmly between the thumb and index finger.

The thumb should be placed behind the neck. The fingers should be placed right behind the frets, not on top of, or in between them.

Standing Position

Sitting Position

Tuning The Guitar

Electronic Tuners:

Many brands of small, battery operated tuners, similar to the one shown below, are available. Simply follow the instructions supplied with your tuner.

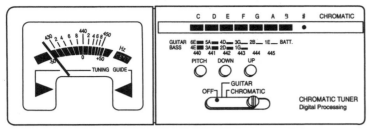

Tuning the Guitar to a piano:

One of the easiest ways to tune a guitar is to a piano keyboard. The six strings of the guitar are tuned to the keyboard notes shown in the following diagram:

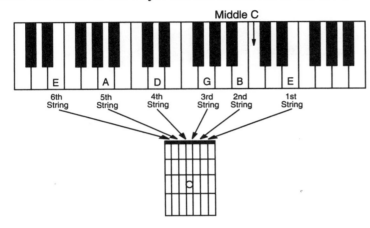

Tuning the Guitar to Itself (Relative Tuning):

1. Tune the 6th string to *E* on the piano (or some other fixed pitch instrument). You can also use a pitch pipe or an electronic guitar tuner.

2. Depress the 6th string at the 5th fret. Play it and you will hear the note *A*, which is the same note as the 5th string open. Turn the 5th string turning key until the pitch of the 5th string matches that of the 6th string.

3. Depress the 5th string at the 5th fret. Play it and you will hear the note *D*, which is the same note as the 4th string open. Turn the 4th string tuning key until the pitch of the 4th string matches that of the 5th string.

4. Depress the 4th string at the 5th fret. Play it and you will hear the note *G*, which is the same note as the 3rd string open. Turn the 3rd string tuning key until the pitch of the 3rd string matches that of the 4th string.

5. Depress the 3rd string at the 4th fret. Play it and you will hear the note *B*, which is the same note as the 2nd string open. Turn the 2nd string tuning key until the pitch of the 2nd string matches that of the 3rd string.

6. Depress the 2nd string at the 5th fret. Play it and you will hear the note *E*, which is the same note as the 1st string open. Turn the 1st string tuning key until the pitch of the 1st string matches that of the 2nd string.

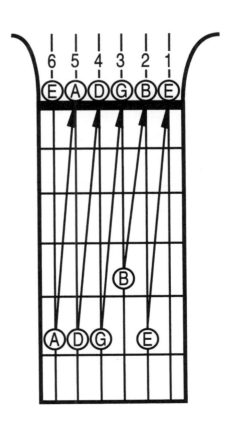

Music Notation

There are seven natural notes. They are named for the first seven letters of the alphabet: A B C D E F G. After G, we begin again with A.

Music is written on a **staff**. The staff consists of five lines with four spaces between the lines:

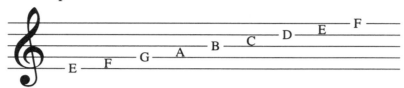

At the beginning of the staff is a treble or G clef. (The treble clef is known as the G clef because it encircles the 2nd line G.) The clef determines the location of notes on the staff. All guitar music is written on a treble clef.

The notes are written on the staff in alphabetical order. The first line is E:

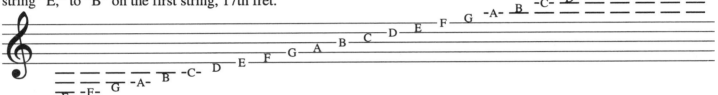

Notes can extend above, and below, the treble clef. When they do, **ledger lines** are added. Following is the approximate range of the guitar from the lowest note, open sixth string "E," to "B" on the first string, 17th fret.

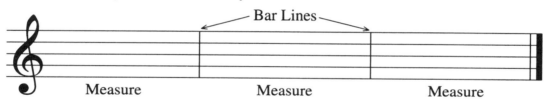

The staff is divided into *measures* by *bar lines*. A heavy double bar line marks the end of the music:

Bar Lines

Measure   Measure   Measure

Tablature is a type of music notation that is specific to the guitar; its use dates back to the 1600's. Tablature illustrates the location of notes on the neck of the guitar. Tablature is usually used in conjunction with a music staff. The notes and rhythms are indicated in the music staff; the tablature shows where those notes are played on the guitar.

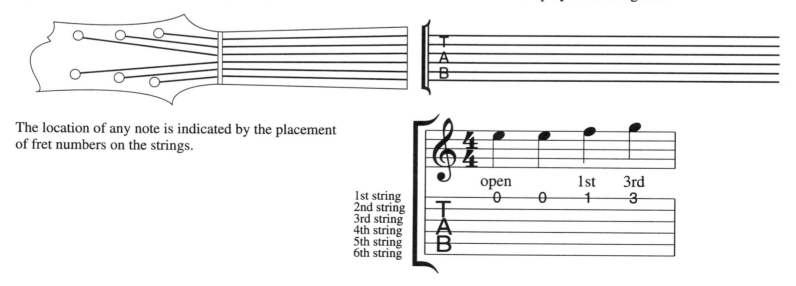

The location of any note is indicated by the placement of fret numbers on the strings.

1st string
2nd string
3rd string
4th string
5th string
6th string

open   1st   3rd

In this book, tablature will be used with all new notes and fingerings. "Tab" will also be used on all pop songs and as an aid to learning the more challenging arrangements; thereby making the learning process easier and more fun.

Rhythm Notation And Time Signatures

At the beginning of every song is a time signature. 4/4 is the most common time signature:

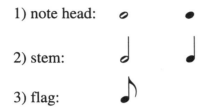

4 FOUR COUNTS TO A MEASURE
4 A QUARTER NOTE RECEIVES ONE COUNT

The top number tells you how many counts per measure.
The bottom number tells you which kind of note receives one count.

The time value of a note is determined by three things:

1) note head: o •

2) stem: ♩ ♩

3) flag: ♪

o This is a whole note. The note head is open and has no stem. In 4/4 time, a whole note receives 4 counts.

♩ This is a half note. It has an open note head and a stem. A half note receives 2 counts.

♩ This is a quarter note. It has a solid note head and a stem. A quarter note receives 1 count.

♪ This is an eighth note. It has a solid note head and a stem with a flag attached. An eighth note receives 1/2 count.

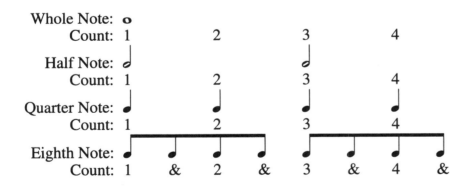

Whole Note: o			
Count: 1	2	3	4
Half Note: ♩		♩	
Count: 1	2	3	4
Quarter Note: ♩	♩	♩	♩
Count: 1	2	3	4
Eighth Note: ♪	♪ ♪	♪ ♪	♪ ♪
Count: 1 &	2 &	3 &	4 &

Count out loud and clap the rhythm to this excerpt from *Jingle Bells*.

Four Counts Per Measure

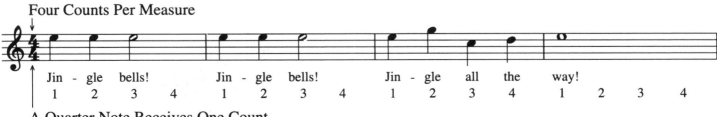

A Quarter Note Receives One Count

The E5 Power Chord

Power chords provide the foundation for rock rhythm guitar. A power chord is a two-note chord voicing, usually played on the bass (low) strings of the guitar. The guitarist's power chords combine with the bass player's part to supply a bottom end to the music that's fat and hard driving.

E5

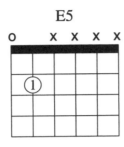

E5

To play the E5, depress the fifth string with the first finger of your left hand at the second fret. To get a good solid tone, make sure the first finger is placed just behind the second fret—not on top of it.

Rhythm Reading:

A whole note gets 4 counts: **o** = 4 counts

A half note gets 2 counts: 𝅗𝅥 = 2 counts

A quarter note gets 1 count: ♩ = 1 count

At the beginning of every song is a **time signature.** 4/4 is the most common time signature:

4 Four Counts To A Measure
4 A Quarter Note Receives One Count

Play all chords with a downstroke (⊓).
(Strike the string with a downward attack of the pick.)

Example 1: E5 Whole Note Study

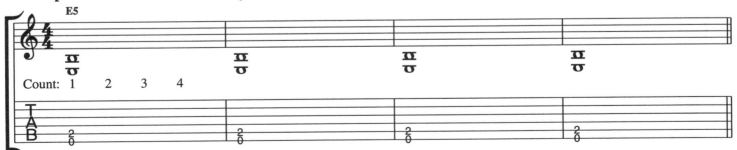

Always count with a steady beat—like the ticking of a clock. Don't slow down, speed up or pause.

Strike the strings with a relaxed, but solid attack. You should hear one clear chord—not two separate notes.

Example 2: E5 Half Note Study

Example 3: E5 Quarter Note Study

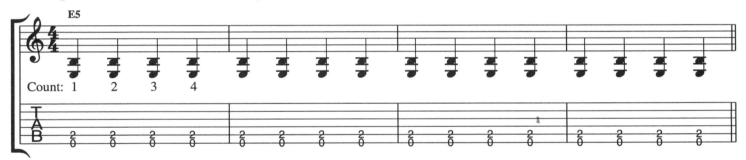

Chord Construction: All power chords are built on two notes: the root (the name of the chord) plus the fifth.

If we number each consecutive note from E to E we get:

E	F	G	A	B	C	D	E
1	2	3	4	**5**	6	7	**8**
(root)				(fifth)			(octave)

$$E + B = E5$$
$$1 + 5 = \text{Power Chord}$$

Chord Forms: The root of the E5 chord is located on the sixth string, therefore, this type of chord form is referred to as **root ⑥** —meaning the root of the chord is on the sixth string. (Strings are indicated by circled numbers.)

There are three basic power chord forms: root⑥, root⑤ and root④. Most guitar chords can be constructed from these three basic forms.

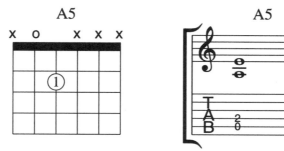

A5

④

Example 4: The A5 Chord

Technique: Be careful not to accidentally strike string ⑥ when playing the A5 chord.

Chord Construction: As you already know, all power chords are built on two notes: the root (the name of the chord) plus the fifth.

If we number each consecutive note from A to A we get:

A	B	C	D	E	F	G	A
1	2	3	4	**5**	6	7	**8**
(root)				(fifth)			(octave)

$$A + E = A5$$

The Root ⑤ Chord Form: The root of the A5 chord is located on the fifth string, therefore, this chord form is referred to as **root ⑤.**

Notice the strong resemblance between the A5 and E5 chords. The chief difference between the two chords is that E5 a root ⑥ form (root on the sixth string) and A5 is a root ⑤ form (root on the fifth string):

A5

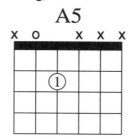

E5

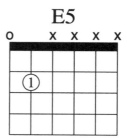

Example 5: Chord Combination Study

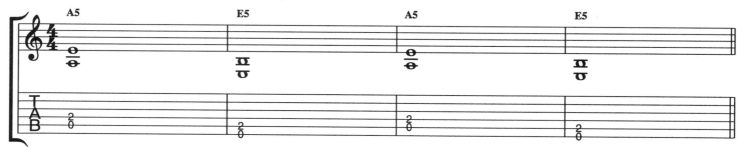

Play the following chord patterns with a solid beat and a strong attack. You should be able
to hear both notes of each chord clearly.

Example 6:

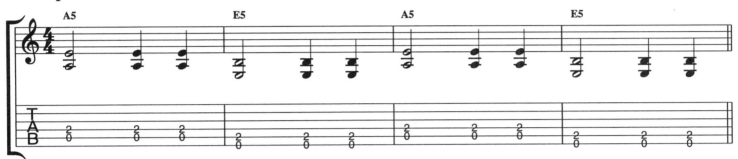

Example 7:

Example 8:

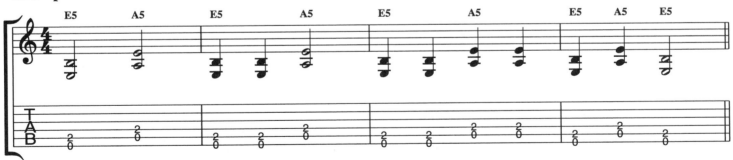

Example 9:

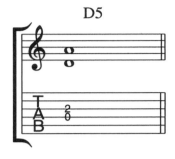

Example 10: The D5 chord

Technique: Be careful not to accidentally strike strings ⑥ and ⑤ when playing the D5 chord.

Chord Construction: The D5, like all power chords, is constructed from the root (D) plus the fifth (A).

If we number each consecutive note from D to D we get:

D	E	F	G	A	B	C	D
1	2	3	4	**5**	6	7	**8**
(root)				(fifth)			(octave)

$$D + A = D5$$

The Root ④ Chord Form: The root (D) of the D5 chord is located on the fourth string, therefore, this type of chord form is referred to as **root ④**.

Example 11:

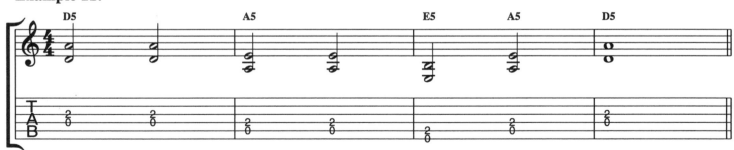

Example 12:

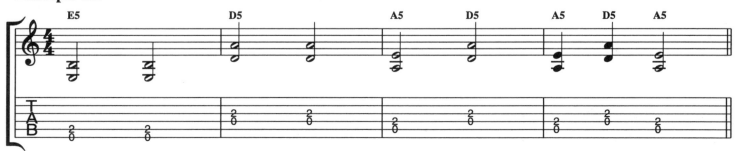

6 Notice the strong resemblance between the E5, A5 and D5 chords. The shape and fingering for each chord is exactly the same:

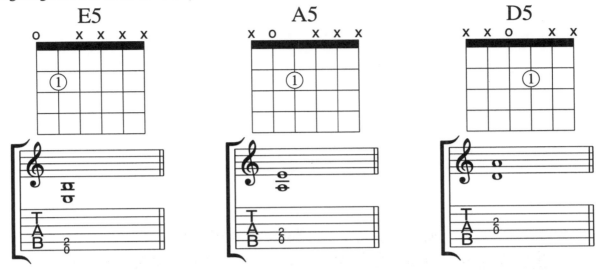

The difference between these three chords, is that each has its root located on a different string:

E5 is a root ⑥ form
A5 is a root ⑤ form
D5 is a root ④ form

As you progress through each level of this method you will derive many chords from these three basic forms.

Example 13

Example 14:

The Blues Progression

 To musicians, the "blues" refers not just to a feel or type of emotion, but to a very specific song form. The blues chord progression is the most common song form found in rock, country, jazz and metal.

The basic blues progression is 12 measures long and consists of 3 chords. In the key of A these 3 chords are: A, D and E. There are many forms and variations of each of these three chords; for now, we will be using only the power chord forms.

Play the following blues progression several times. Does it sound familiar? Try to anticipate the sound of each upcoming chord change.

The 12-bar
Blues Progression

Example 15

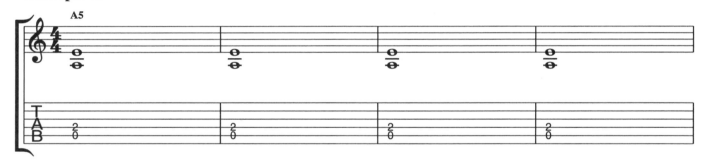

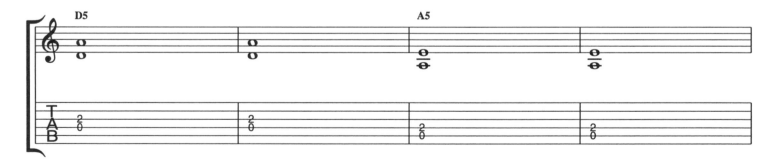

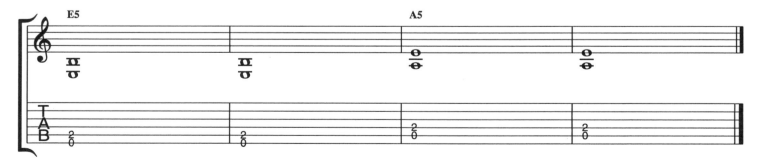

Heavy double bar lines (⫸) are used to mark the end of a song.

Understanding the Blues Progression: The three basic chords in a blues progression are always the I (first), IV (fourth) and V (fifth) chords in the key. To show their relationship to the key, chords are often indicated with Roman numerals.

Here is a seven-note scale built on A. You can see that A is the I chord, D is the IV and E is the V chord.

Scale:	A	B	C	D	E	F	G	A
Scale Steps:	**1**	2	3	**4**	**5**	6	7	**8**
Chord Function:	**I**			**IV**	**V**			

The basic chord changes (I, IV and V) in a 12-bar blues always occur at the same point in the progression:

While playing the following blues progression, note how the location of each chord matches the preceding diagram.

Example 16

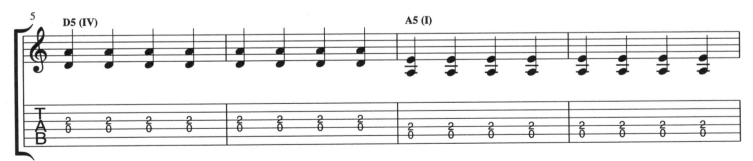

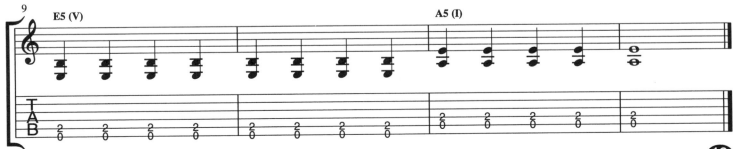

9

The 12-bar blues progression can be broken down into three sections, **called phrases,** of four bars each. The more familiar you become with each of these three phrases the easier it will be to recognize the sound of the blues progression and its many variations.

Example 17

The first phrase (bars 1–4) is based on four bars of the I chord:

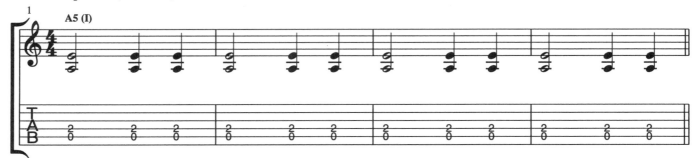

Example 18

The second phrase (bars 5–8) begins with two bars of the IV chord followed by two bars of the I chord:

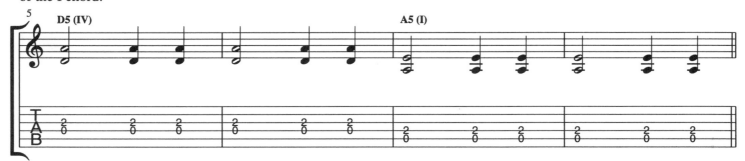

Example 19

The third phrase (bars 9–12) begins with two bars of the V chord, which then resolves to two bars of the I chord:

10 The following example shows the three phrases combined into one 12-bar progression. Note where each chord change takes place. These basics remain the same in all blues progressions—whether played by B. B. King, the Stones, Stevie Ray Vaughan, ZZ Top or Led Zeppelin.

Example 20

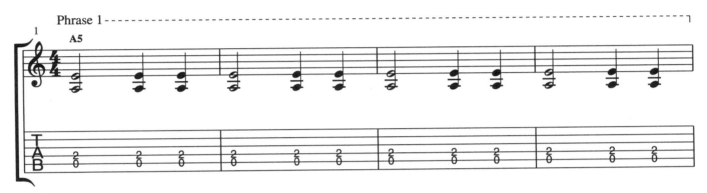

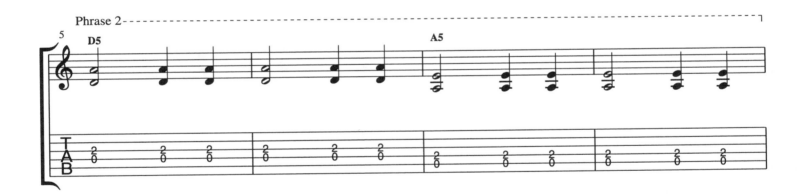

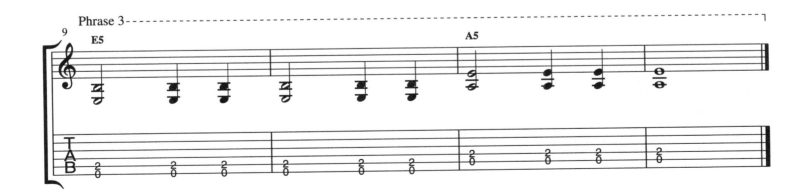

The Eighth Note Rhythm

11 This is an eighth note: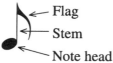

Two eighth notes equal one quarter note: ♫ = ♩

Single eighth notes are written like this: ♪

In groups of two or more, eighth notes are beamed together: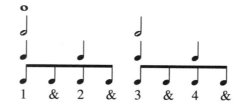

Counting Eighth Notes: In $\frac{4}{4}$ time, each measure is divided into four equal beats. Eighth notes divide each beat in half. Beats can be divided in half by saying "and" in between each count.

Count out loud in the following example. Tap your foot on each count (1 2 3 4). Your foot should come down on the counts and up on each "and."

Example 21

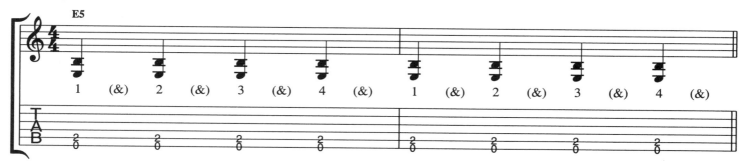

Now play on "and." Continue to count out loud and tap your foot. The chords that fall on the downbeats (1 2 3 4) should be accented (emphasized by striking just a little harder). This is indicated with an accent mark (>). Remember the "ands" come in between the counts.

Example 22

This next example combines eighth notes and each of the three power chords.

Example 23

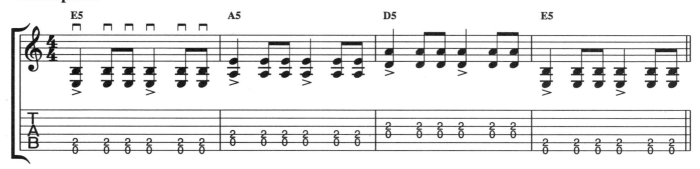

Muted Blues uses a new technique: **The Palm Mute.** Gently lay the palm of your pick hand on the bridge of your guitar. If your hand is too far in front of the bridge, the strings will be too muted; too far behind and the strings will not be muted enough. The palm mute produces a short, muffled percussive attack which adds rhythmic drive and intensity to your playing. On the accented chords you should lessen the palm mute by lifting your palm slightly off the bridge. The palm mute effect is indicated by the abbreviation: **P.M.**

Muted Blues

Example 24

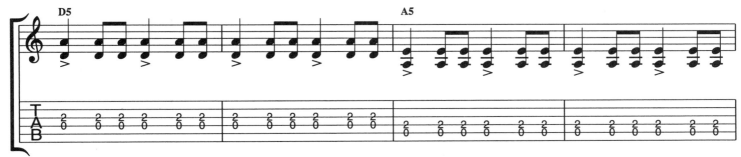

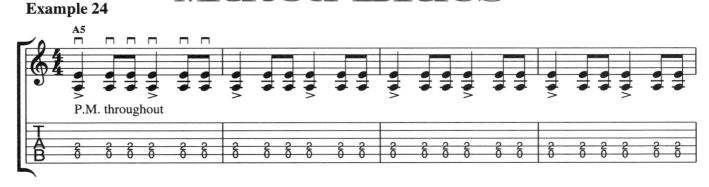

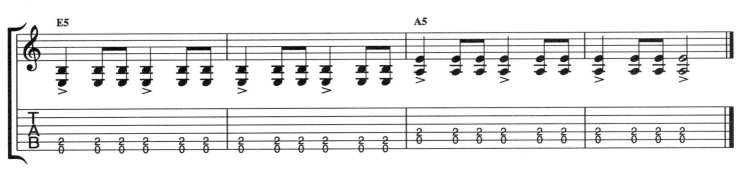

13 Each of the three power chord forms (root ⑥, root ⑤ and root ④) can be expanded to three note voicings. The added note is the root doubled one octave higher. Let's start with the E5 root ⑥ form.

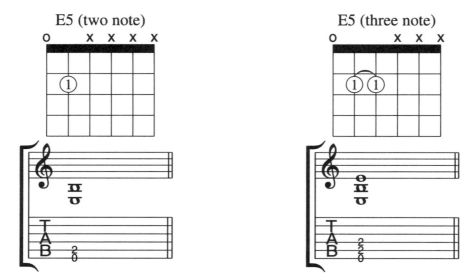

The One Finger Barre: When one finger is used to depress two or more strings at once.

The E5 requires a barre at the second fret. Lay your first finger across both the fourth and fifth strings and press both strings to the fretboard, just behind the fret. Turn the first finger a little to the side, so the bony part of your finger, rather than the softer, fleshy part comes in contact with the string. Place your left hand thumb directly behind the neck to add strength to your hand.

Push your pick straight through the sixth, fifth and fourth strings, bringing it to rest on the third string. This will insure that you do not accidentally strike the open third, second and first strings.

Example 25

Chord Construction: All power chords are two-note chords (the root + fifth). The three-note power chord contains the root (1), plus the fifth (5), plus the root doubled an octave higher (8). Doubling the root gives the three-note power chord a bigger sound than the two-note voicing; but does not change its fundamental quality of being a power chord.

E	F	G	A	B	C	D	E
1	2	3	4	5	6	7	8
(root)				(fifth)			(octave)

E + B + E = E5 (three-note form)
1 + 5 + 8 = Three Note Power Chord

14 Now let's expand the root ⑤ form of the A power chord from a two to a three-note voicing. The A5 voicing also requires a first finger barre at the second fret, just like the three-note E5.

A5 (two note)
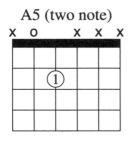
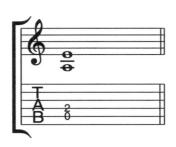

A5 (three note)
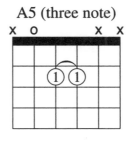
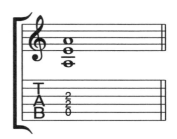

Example 26

Technique: To avoid striking unwanted strings, push your pick straight through the fifth, fourth and third strings, bringing it to rest on the second string.

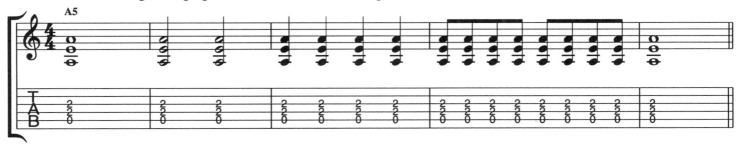

Chord Construction: The three-note A5 contains the root (1) plus the fifth (5) plus the root doubled an octave higher (8).

A	B	C	D	E	F	G	A
1	2	3	4	**5**	6	7	**8**
(root)				(fifth)			(octave)

A + E + A = A5 (three-note form)

Compare the three-note A5 and E5 voicings. They both look alike and are fingered alike. The difference is that A5 is a root ⑤ form and E5 is a root ⑥ form.

A5
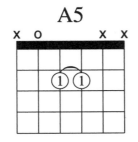

E5
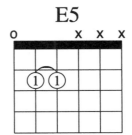

Example 27: Chord Combination Study

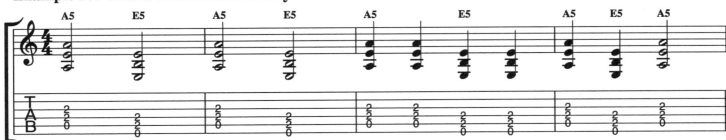

Three Note Power Chords

Now let's expand the root ④ form of the D power chord from a two to a three-note voicing. The chord shape of the three-note D5 is different from the shape of the three-note E5 and A5. This is because the third and second strings are tuned to a different interval than the rest of the guitar strings.

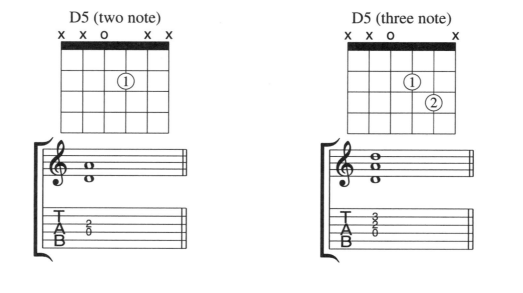

Example 28

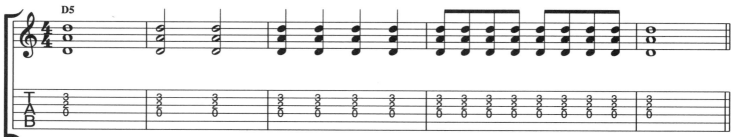

Chord Construction:

D	E	F	G	A	B	C	D
1	2	3	4	**5**	6	7	**8**
(root)				(fifth)			(octave)

D + A + D = D5 (three-note form)

Example 29: Chord Combination Study

This next example combines two and three-note power chords in a blues progression with a hard rock feel.

Hard Rock Blues

Example 30:

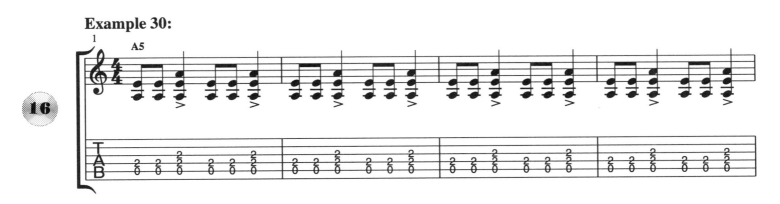

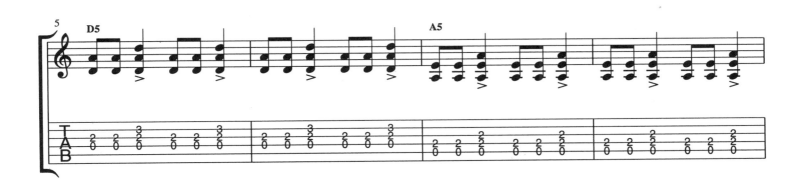

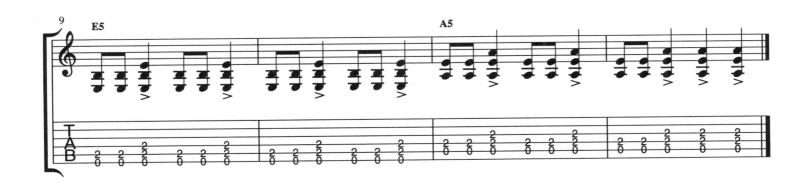

As a lead guitarist you will be playing melodies and improvised solos. Start by getting familiar with the natural notes (no sharps or flats) in the first position (the first four frets).

This diagram shows all of the natural notes in first position. Beginning with the low E, play each note, from the low E to the high G on the first string (play all notes in alphabetical order). Say the notes out loud as you play.

Now let's work on each string separately.

Example 31: Notes on the Sixth String

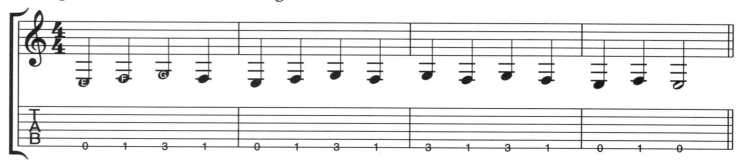

Example 32: Notes on the Fifth String

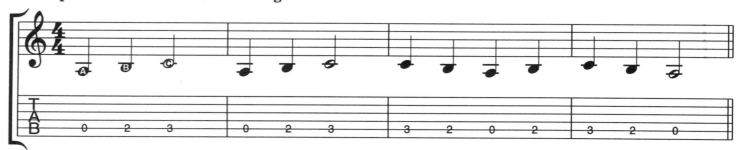

Example 33: Notes on the Fourth String

Example 34: Notes on the Third String

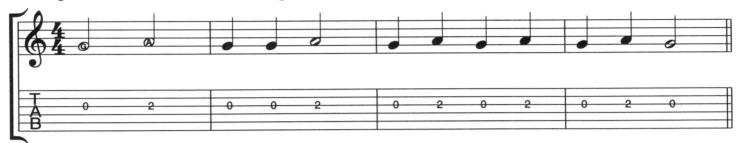

Example 35: Notes on the Second String

Example 36: Notes on the First String

Example 37: Notes on all Six Strings

Learning to read music requires a great deal of practice. For more on single note reading see *Guitar Method 1* of *Belwin's 21st Century Guitar Library*.

Good rhythm guitar parts often consist of more than chords alone. A **rhythm riff** is a repetitive figure that usually outlines the chord changes. It could be a mixture of single-notes and chords, a bass line pattern or a single-note figure. In this section we will be looking at several different examples of rhythm riffs.

The Minor Pentatonic Scale is the most common scale used in rock guitar. All pentatonic scales contain five notes (penta means five). In the following diagrams, see how similar the "shape," or pattern, of the E minor pentatonic scale is to the "shape" of the E5 power chord. The E minor pentatonic scale contains all the notes in the E5 power chord (E - B - E). Like the E5, this scale fingering has its root, or **tonic** note, on the sixth string.

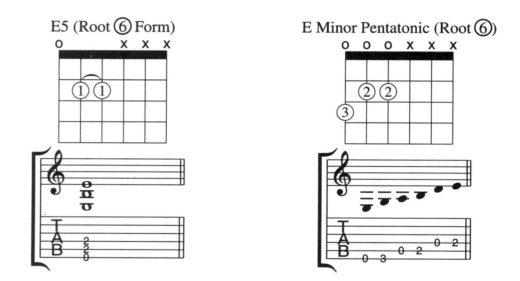

Play the chord and then the scale. Listen for how the notes sound in relation to the chord.

Example 38:

Example 39:

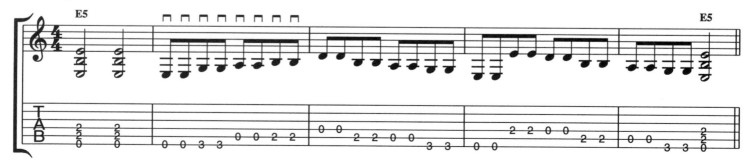

The combination of down and upstrokes is called **alternate picking.** At slower tempos, playing with all downstrokes can be very effective. Downstrokes pack a lot of punch and can really add drive to a rhythm or lead part. But for faster playing you must develop both down and upstrokes.

The Down-Upstroke: Think of the down-upstroke as one continuous movement—a note is played with a downstroke, then as the pick comes back up, returning to its original playing position, strike the next note with the upward motion of the pick. The pick hand should swing freely from the wrist in a slight arc.

Eighth notes are often played with alternating down-upstrokes. Down on the counts (1 2 3 4) and up on "and."

Here are three common rock bass line patterns, experiment with both alternate picking and all downstrokes.

Example 40

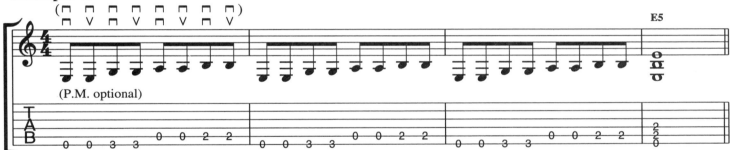

This next pattern is a variation on Example 40. In this one you have to play a downstroke on the fifth string B, followed by an upstroke on the fourth string D.

Example 41

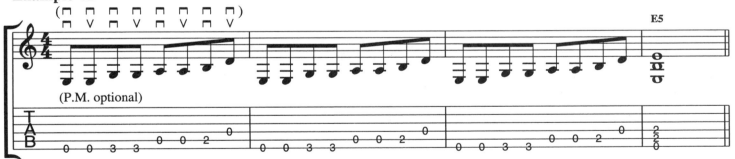

Example 42

20 Now let's take the E minor pentatonic scale and transpose it to A. The A minor pentatonic is played on the fifth, fourth, and third strings. Notice that the basic shape of the A minor pentatonic scale is exactly the same as the E minor pentatonic, except the root of the scale is on the fifth string.

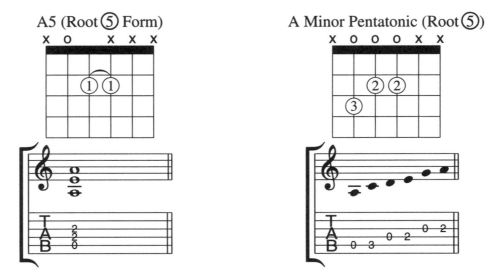

A5 (Root ⑤ Form)   A Minor Pentatonic (Root ⑤)

Play the chord and then the scale. Listen for how the notes sound in relation to the chord.

Example 43

Example 44
(Example 40 transposed to A)

(P.M. optional)

Example 45
(Example 41 transposed to A)

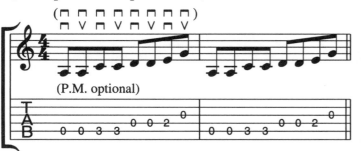

(P.M. optional)

Example 46
(Example 42 transposed to A)

(P.M. optional)

Now let's transpose the minor pentatonic scale to D. The D minor pentatonic is fingered on the fourth, third and second strings and has its root on string ④. Like the three-note D power chord, the shape and fingering for this scale remains the same as the E and A scales except for the notes on the second string. This is because the third and second strings are tuned to a different interval than the rest of the guitar strings.

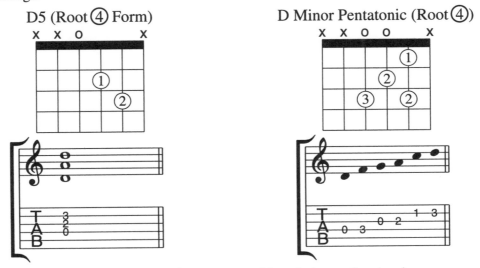

Play the chord and then the scale. Listen for how the notes sound in relation to the chord.

Example 47

Example 48
(Example 40 transposed to D)

(P.M. optional)

Example 49
(Example 41 transposed to D)

(P.M. optional)

Example 50
(Example 42 transposed to D)

(P.M. optional)

A riff pattern works over a specific chord. Often the whole pattern can be transposed to work over every chord in the blues progression. Each riff and pattern will first be presented in "E." They will then be transposed to work over the A and D chords. **All of the classic rock rhythm riffs used in this section are derived from the minor pentatonic scale.**

This first riff is inspired by Led Zeppelin's *Heartbreaker*.

Example 51: Riff 1

Now transpose Riff 1 to A. Notice that although the riff pattern is played on the next string group, the fingering pattern remains exactly the same.

Example 52: Riff 1 transposed to A

Now transpose Riff 1 to D. Again, notice that although the riff pattern changes to another string group, the fingering pattern remains exactly the same.

Example 53: Riff 1 transposed to D

Now play Riff 1, in the context of a 12-bar blues progression.

Broken Hearted

Example 54

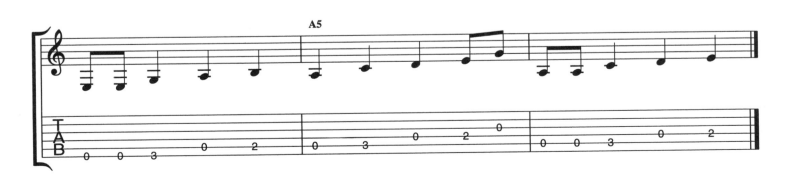

Tied Notes: A curved line connecting two notes of the same pitch is called a *tie*. Play the first note and hold it for the time value of both notes combined:

Riff 2 (and countless variations of it) is the basis for hundreds of rock tunes including *Crossroads,* the Robert Johnson tune made famous by Eric Clapton and Cream. First learn this riff with all downstrokes. When you're comfortable with the riff, try the optional alternate picking pattern.

Example 55: Riff 2

Now transpose Riff 2 to A. Notice that although the riff pattern is played on the next string group, the fingering pattern remains exactly the same.

Example 56: Riff 2 transposed to A

Now transpose Riff 2 to D. Notice the fingering differences between this example and its counterparts in E and A. **All fingering patterns shift one fret higher when transposed to the second string.**

Example 57: Riff 2 transposed to D

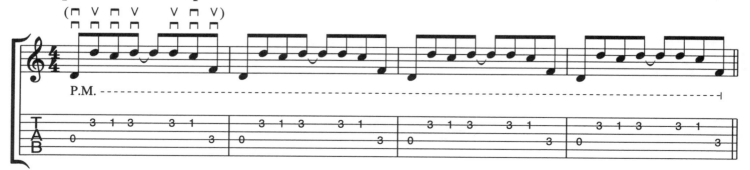

Now play Riff 2 in the context of a 12-bar blues progression.

Georgia Roads

Example 58

Many riffs contain chord fragments that add extra power to the part. There are two, two-note chord fragments in the following riff. The first is part of the E5 power chord and should be played with a first finger barre. The second chord fragment is a type of D5 power chord consisting of the open A and D strings played together. Riff 3 is based on the main riff from ZZ Top's *Got Me Under Pressure*.

Example 59: Riff 3

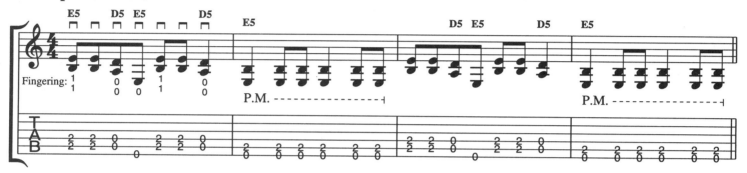

When transposed to A, the first chord fragment in this riff is from the A5 power chord and is played with a first finger barre. The second chord fragment is an open string voicing of G5.

Example 60: Riff 3 transposed to A

When transposed to D, the first chord fragment in this riff is from the D5 power chord and the second chord fragment is a two-note C5. Follow the indicated fingerings.

Example 61: Riff 3 transposed to D

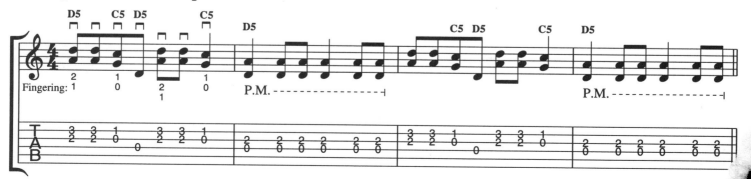

High Pressure Drive

Example 62

Riff 4 is the foundation for one of the greatest rock and roll tunes of all time, *Jumpin' Jack Flash* by the Stones. The two-note chord fragment is part of the E5 power chord and should be played with a first finger barre.

Example 63: Riff 4

When transposed to A, the two-note chord fragment is part of the A5 power chord and should be played with a first finger barre.

Example 64: Riff 4 transposed to A

When transposed to D, the two-note chord fragment is part of the D5 power chord. Note the indicated fingering.

Example 65: Riff 4 transposed to D

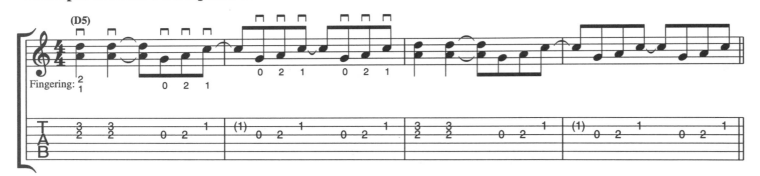

When used in the context of a 12-bar blues, Riff 4, the *Jumpin' Jack Flash* riff, becomes an excellent example of combining power chords and single note lines over each of the chord changes.

The Jack Flash Riff

Example 66

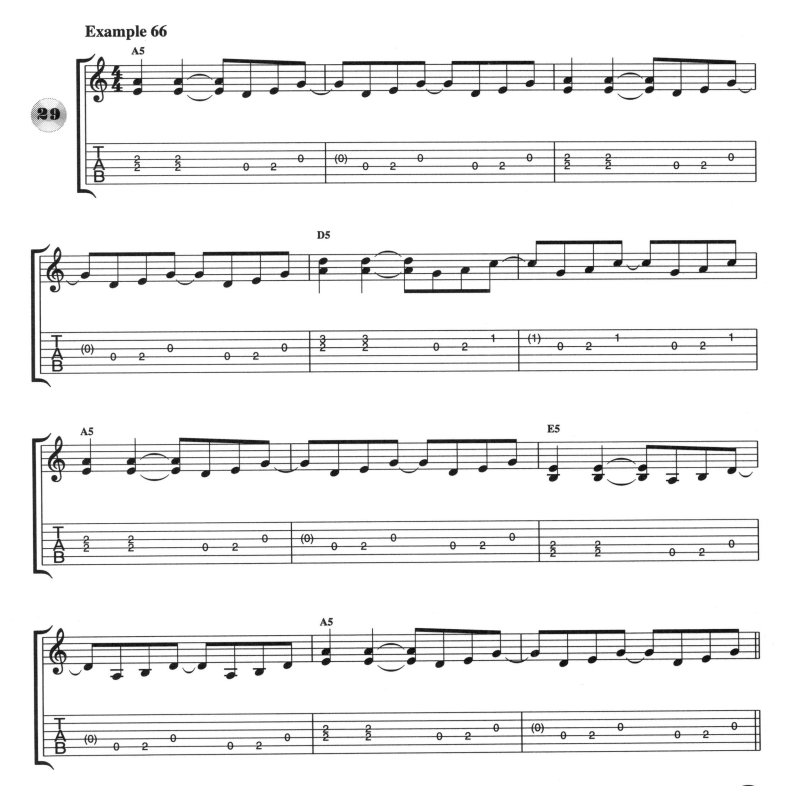

Target Tones: Not all rhythm riffs must be transposed for each chord. Often the same effect can be achieved by playing the same riff over every chord, altering only the last note—*the target tone.* Usually the target tone is the root of the chord. The target tone concept will become especially important in the section on *Lead Riffs.*

Rhythm Riff 5 is based on Buddy Guy's *Mary Had a Little Lamb,* a staple in Stevie Ray Vaughan's repertoire. First try the riff over the A chord. The target tone is the last note of the riff and is the root of the chord (A).

The Rest: A rest marks a period of silence. For every type of note (eighth, quarter, half, whole, etc.) there is an equivalent rest. Rhythm Riff 5 begins with an eighth note rest. Count it as you would any eighth note and then begin playing on the "and" of 1.

$$\text{Eighth Rest:} \quad \text{y} \quad = \quad \text{♪} \quad = 1/2 \text{ count}$$

Example 67: Rhythm Riff 5 (with A as the target tone)

Notes played before the first complete measure are **pick-up notes.** This riff begins with one measure of pick-up notes leading into the target tone, which is played on the first beat of each chord change.

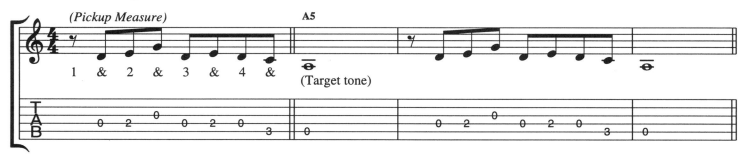

This next example shows Rhythm Riff 5 played over the D chord. Note that only the target tone has changed.

Example 68: Rhythm Riff 5 (with D as the target tone)

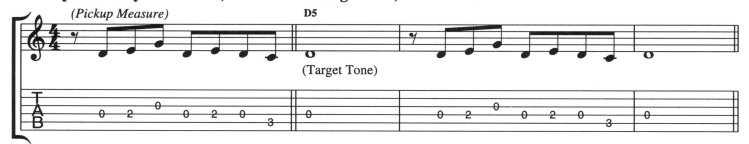

Example 69: Rhythm Riff 5 (with E as the target tone)

Now try Rhythm Riff 5 over the entire 12-bar blues form. Notice how the pick-up bar leads into each chord change.

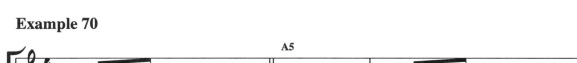

Quarter Rest: ♩ = 1 count

Half Rest: ♩ = 2 counts

Buddy's Blues

Example 70

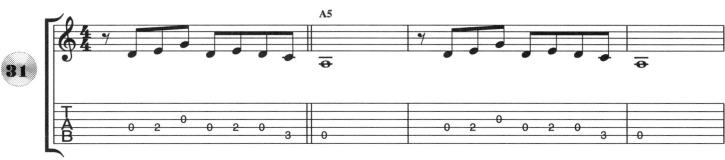

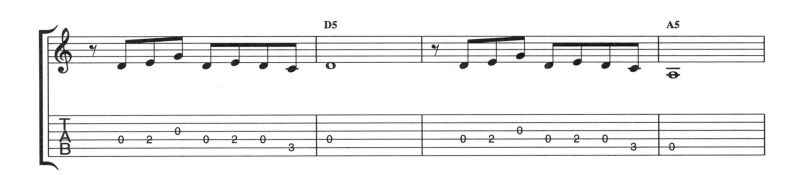

The Major Scale

 Before you can explore rhythm or lead guitar in more depth, you will need a good understanding of the major scale and how it is constructed.

1) All major scales contain seven consecutive notes.
2) All major scales are constructed from the following pattern (a whole-step is two frets and a half-step is one fret).

Major Scale Construction:

whole	whole	half	whole	whole	whole	half
1	1	1/2	1	1	1	1/2

Play the C major scale, on the second string of the guitar. Note the sequence of whole and half steps. You can use whatever fingering is easiest. The point is to locate the notes and to visualize the pattern: 1 1 1/2 1 1 1 1/2

Example 71: The C Major Scale

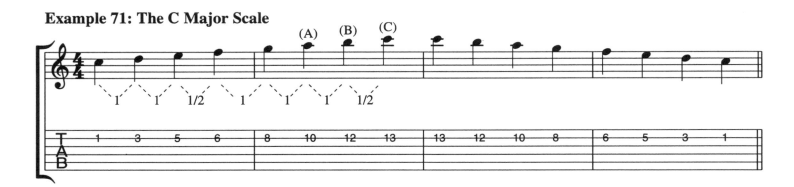

Sharp (♯) and Flat (♭) Signs: A sharp sign raises a note one half step (up to the next fret). A flat sign lowers a note one half step (down to the next lower fret). As you learn to spell each of the major scales you will see that some require flat notes and others sharp notes. (The first four scales you will study use only sharps.)

Play the G major scale on the third string. Notice the F♯, you can see that the F♯ is required to complete the pattern of whole and half-steps.

Example 72: The G Major Scale

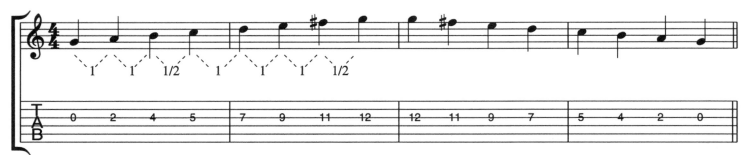

The D major scale contains both F♯ and C♯. Play it on the fourth string.

Example 73: The D Major Scale

The A major scale contains three sharps: F♯, C♯ and G♯.

Example 74: The A Major Scale

The E major scale contains four sharps: F♯, C♯, G♯ and D♯.

Example 75: The E Major Scale

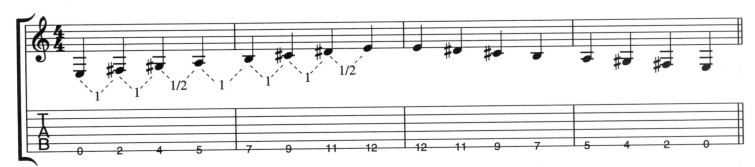

33 Rock's most popular rhythm guitar figure is the "boogie" pattern. From T-Bone Walker and Fats Domino, to Chuck Berry and Elvis, to the Beatles, the Stones, Led Zeppelin and just about every rock band in existence—they've all played this pattern.

The foundation of the boogie pattern is the alternation between a two-note power chord and a two-note sixth chord.

E5 is built from the root (1) and fifth (5) of the E major scale:

E Major Scale:	**E**	**F♯**	**G♯**	**A**	**B**	**C♯**	**D♯**	**E**
E5 Chord Tones:	1				5			

E6 is built from the root and sixth of the E major scale:

E Major Scale:	**E**	**F♯**	**G♯**	**A**	**B**	**C♯**	**D♯**	**E**
E6 Chord Tones:	1					6		

Compare the fingerings for the E5 and E6. *Do not lift your first finger off of string ⑤ when playing the E6 chord.*

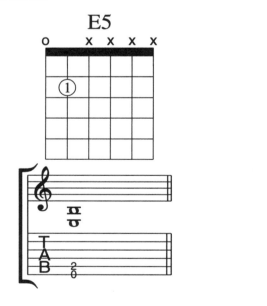

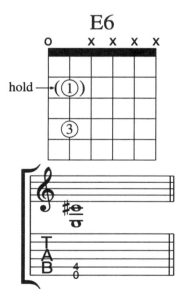

Example 76: The Basic "E" Boogie Pattern

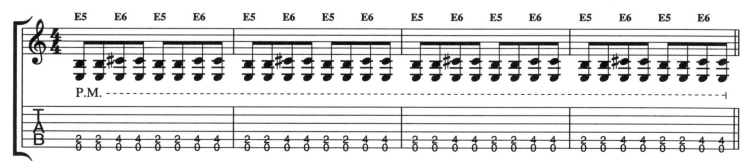

34 Now we will transpose the boogie pattern to the root ⑤ A chord.

A5 is built from the root and fifth of the A major scale:

A Major Scale:	A	B	C♯	D	E	F♯	G♯	A
A5 Chord Tones:	1				5			

A6 is built from the root and sixth of the A major scale:

A Major Scale:	A	B	C♯	D	E	F♯	G♯	A
A6 Chord Tones:	1					6		

Compare the fingerings for A5 and A6. *Do not lift your first finger off of string ④ when playing the A6 chord.*

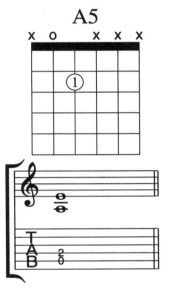

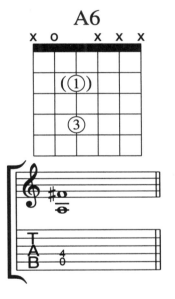

Example 77: The Basic "A" Boogie Pattern

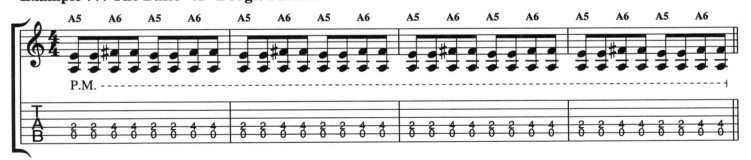

The next example combines the E and A boogie patterns.

Example 78

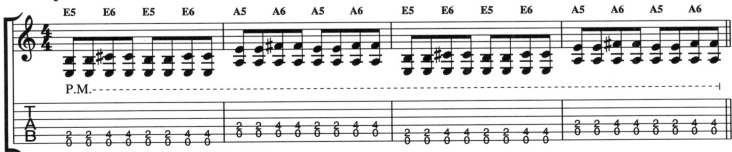

Now let's transpose the boogie pattern to the root ④ D chord.

D5 is built from the root and fifth of the D major scale:

D Major Scale:	D	E	F♯	G	A	B	C♯	D
D5 Chord Tones:	1				5			

D6 is built from the root and sixth of the D major scale:

D Major Scale:	D	E	F♯	G	A	B	C♯	D
D6 Chord Tones:	1					6		

Compare the fingerings for D5 and D6. *Do not lift your first finger off of string ③ when playing the D6 chord.*

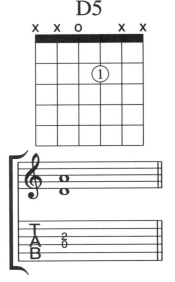

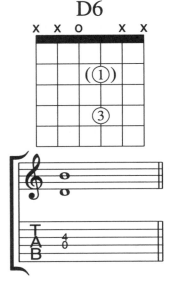

Example 79: The Basic "D" Boogie Pattern

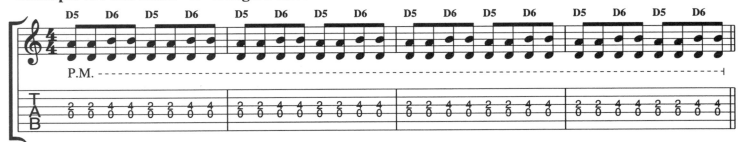

The next example combines the E, A and D boogie patterns.

Example 80

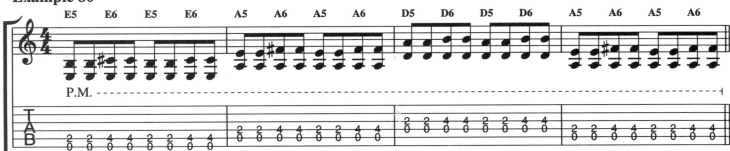

36

Now try a complete 12-bar blues boogie progression. Notice the move to the IV chord (D) in the second measure. This is an extremely common variation on the basic pattern. Also, the change to the V chord (E) in the twelfth measure is a simple "turn-around" which is designed to bring you back to the beginning. Practice this pattern with, and without, a palm mute.

Repeat signs, First and Second Endings:

The Boogie Pattern

Example 81

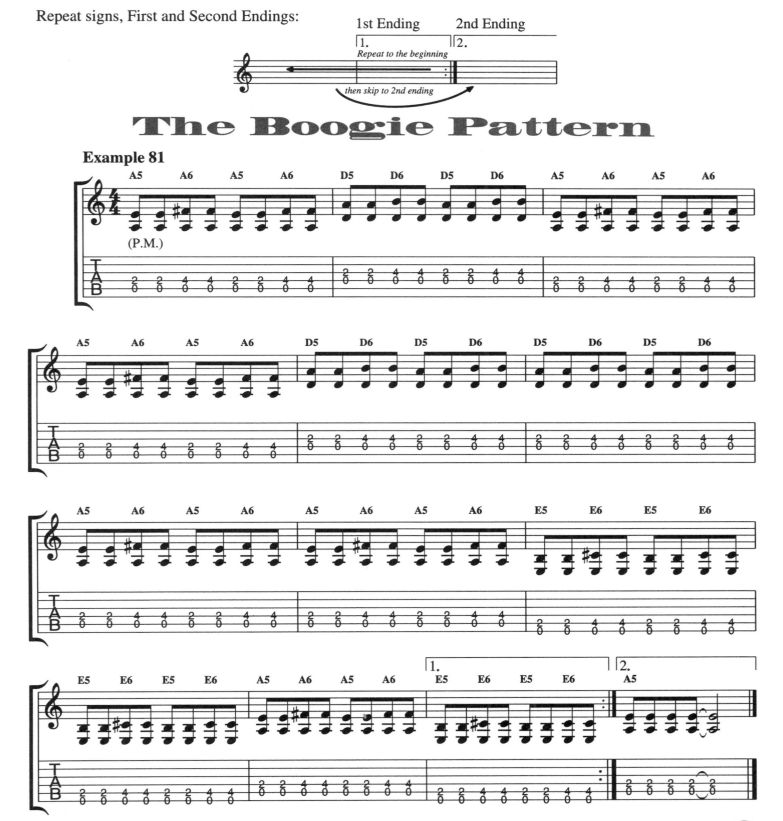

37

The boogie pattern has hundreds of variations. The next example demonstrates one of the most popular rhythmic variations on the basic boogie pattern. Rather than changing chords on each beat (1 2 3 4), some of the chords in this pattern change on "off beats" (on "and"). Also notice that the first chord in each measure is **anticipated**—played on the "and" of 4, instead of on 1.

Example 82: The "E" Boogie Pattern, Variation 1

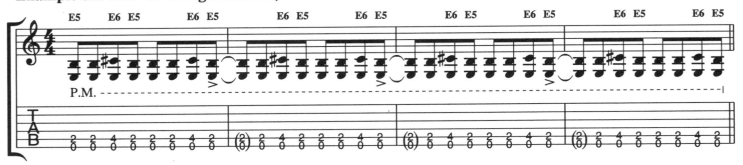

Now try the same pattern over the A chord.

Example 83: The "A" Boogie Pattern, Variation 1

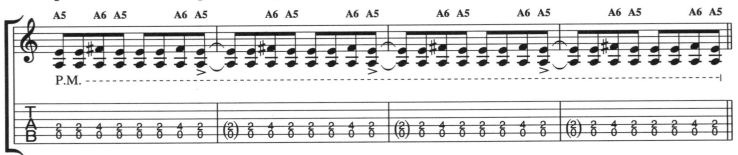

Now try the same pattern over the D chord.

Example 84: The "D" Boogie Pattern, Variation 1

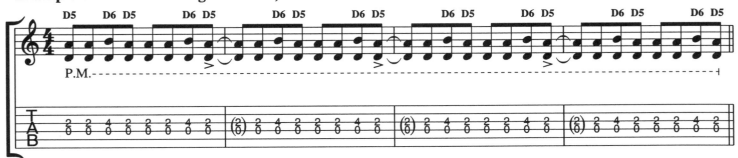

Now play Variation 1 over the entire 12-bar blues form. Use all downstrokes and accent each anticipated chord. You should also try playing with, and without, a palm mute.

Variation 1

Example 85

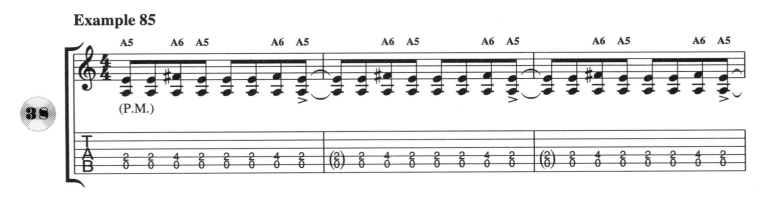

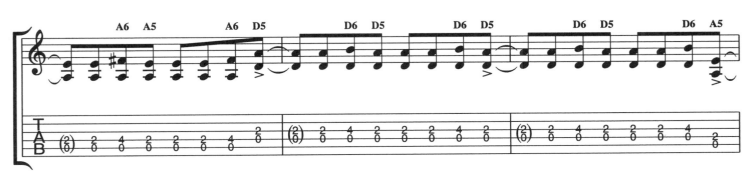

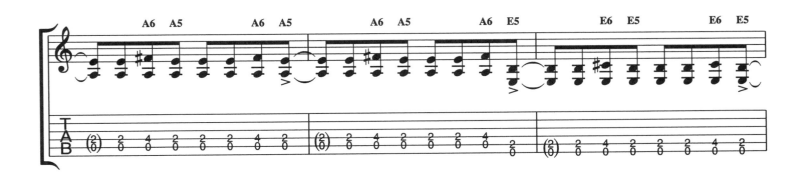

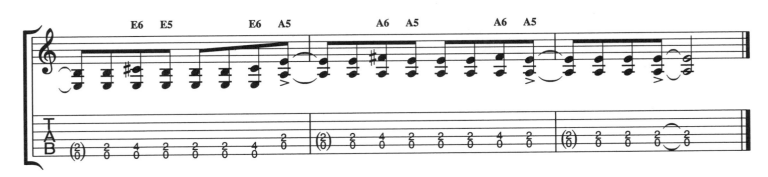

Variation 2 adds a two-note seventh chord to the pattern.

39 The two-note voicing for E7 is built from the **root** and **flatted seventh (♭7)** *of the E major scale.* Since a flat lowers a note one-half step, if the seventh note of the major scale is sharp then the flatted seventh would be natural (D♯ becomes D♮).

Chord Contruction of Two-Note E7:

E Major Scale:	E	F♯	G♯	A	B	C♯	D♯	E
	1	2	3	4	5	6	7	8

All Two-Note 7th Chords = 1 + ♭7

E7 = E + D(♮)

Compare the fingerings for E5, E6 and E7. *Do not lift your first finger off string* ⑤ *when playing either the E6 or E7 chord.*

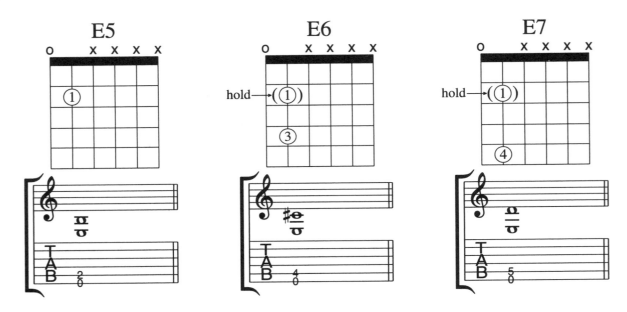

Example 86: Combining the E5, E6 and E7 Chords (Variation 2)

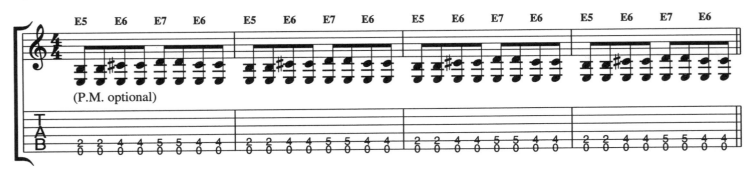

40 Now transfer Variation 2 to the root ⑤ A chord. The two-note voicing for A7 is built from the root and flatted seventh (♭7) of the A major scale (G♯ becomes G♮).

Chord Contruction of Two-Note A7:

A Major Scale: A   B   C♯   D   E   F♯   G♯   A
                1   2   3   4   5   6   7   8

All Two-Note 7th Chords = 1 + ♭7

A7 = A + G(♮)

Compare the fingerings for A5, A6 and A7. *Do not lift your first finger off string ④ when playing either the A6 or A7 chord.*

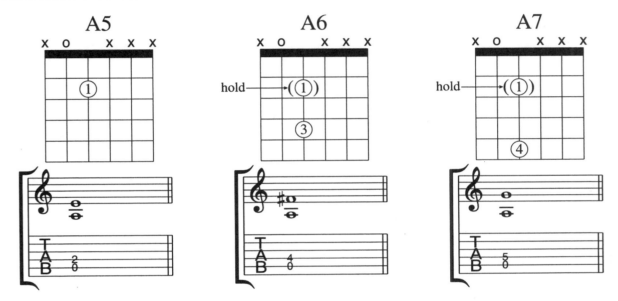

Example 87: Combining the A5, A6 and A7 chords

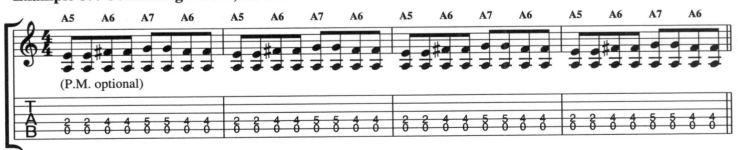

Example 88: Combining the New "E" and "A" Boogie Patterns

41 Now transfer Variation 2 to the root ④ D chord. The two-note voicing for D7 is built from the root and flatted seventh (♭7) of the D major scale (C# becomes C♮).

Chord Contruction of Two-Note D7:

D Major Scale:	D	E	F#	G	A	B	C#	D
	1	2	3	4	5	6	7	8

All Two-Note 7th Chords = 1 + ♭7

D7 = D + C(♮)

Compare the fingerings for D5, D6 and D7. *Do not lift your first finger off string ③ when playing either the D6 or D7 chord.*

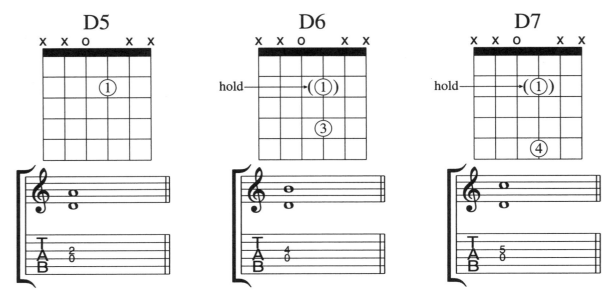

Example 89: Combining the D5, D6 and D7 chords

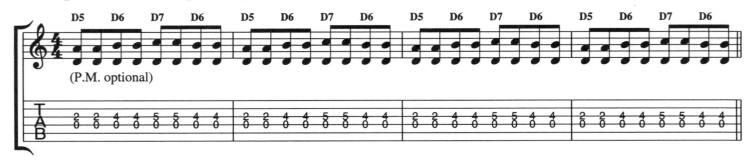

Example 90: Variation 2 Over E, A and D

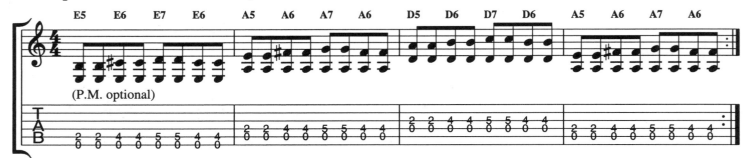

Now play Variation 2 over the entire 12-bar blues form. Use all downstrokes and try
playing with, and without, a palm mute.

Boogie Pattern
Variation 2

Example 91

The Boogie Pattern: Variation 3

Variation 3 is a rhythmic variation similar to Variation 1, only incorporating the seventh chord into the pattern. As in Variation 1, rather than changing chords on each beat (1 2 3 4), some of the chords in this pattern change on "off beats." Again, the first chord in each measure is anticipated (played on the "and" of 4, instead of on 1). Try each example with and without a palm mute.

Example 92: The "E" Boogie Pattern, Variation 3

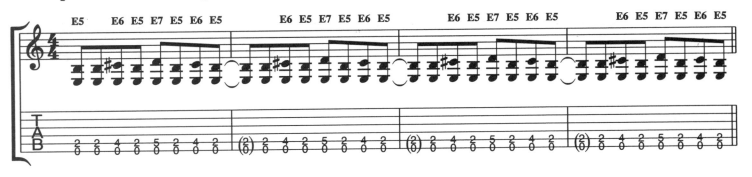

Now transpose the pattern to the root ⑤ A chord.

Example 93: The "A" Boogie Pattern, Variation 3

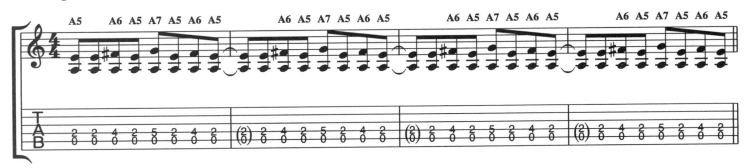

Now transpose the pattern to the root ④ D chord.

Example 94: The "D" Boogie Pattern, Variation 3

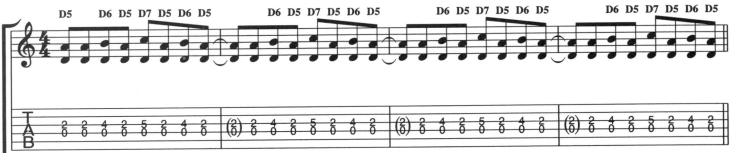

Now play Variation 3 over the entire 12-bar blues form. Use all downstrokes and accent each anticipated chord. Again, try playing with, and without, a palm mute.

Boogie Pattern, Variation 3

Example 95

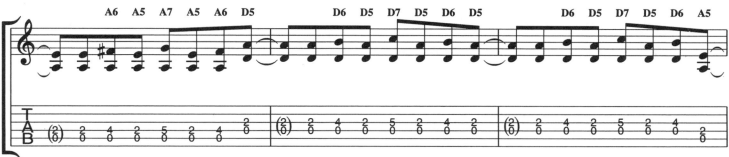

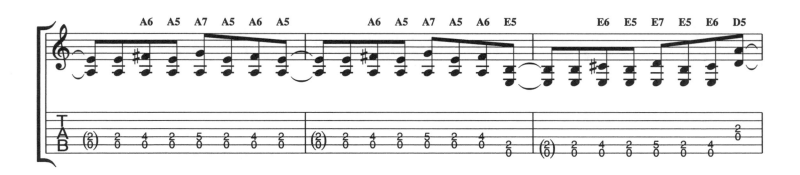

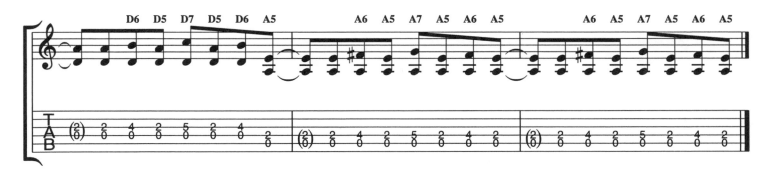

Variation 4 is a syncopated variation with the addition of a single note riff. The added single notes are the minor third (♭3) to the major third (3) of the chord. Try each example with, and without, a palm mute.

A Major Scale:	A	B	C♯	D	E	F♯	G♯	A
	1	2	3	4	5	6	7	8

The major third of the A chord is C♯, therefore the minor third (♭3) is C♮.

Hammer-ons: Not all notes are struck with a pick. Often notes are sounded with the left hand alone. In the next example, G is connected to G♯ with a curved line called a slur marking (⌢). Play the G with your second finger, then sound the G♯ by "hammering" your third finger down onto the fret. Do not strike the string with your pick. Keep your hand relaxed and don't hammer too hard. This technique is a lot easier than it might first appear. It is a very important technique to master.

Example 96: The "E" Boogie Pattern, Variation 4

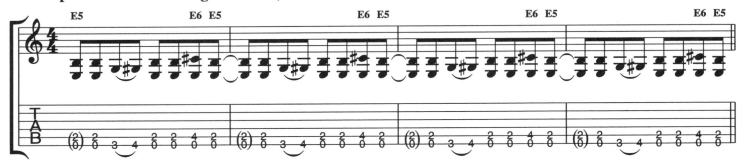

Now transpose the pattern to the root ⑤ A chord.

Example 97: The "A" Boogie Pattern, Variation 4

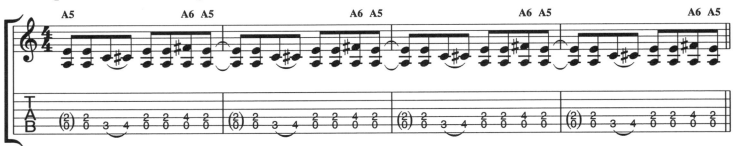

Now transpose it to the root ④ D chord.

Example 98: The "D" Boogie Pattern, Variation 4

Now play Variation 4 over the entire 12-bar blues form. Note the ending lick in the last two bars. This lick uses all the notes of the A minor pentatonic scale (page 26).

Chord Symbols: Rather than cluttering the music by notating every chord form with a chord symbol (A5, A6, A7, etc.), it is common to indicate the overall harmony with only one chord symbol. The indicated chord symbols for a blues progression are usually I7, IV7 and V7 (in the key of A: A7, D7 and E7).

Boogie Pattern, Variation 4

Example 99

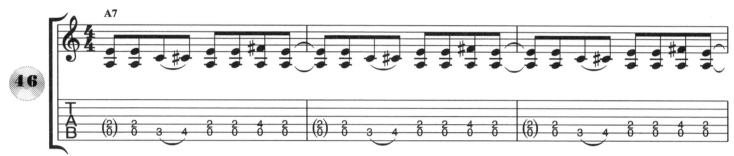

The Boogie Pattern: Variation 5

Variation 5 uses all the techniques studied so far and is based on Led Zeppelin's classic: *Rock and Roll.* This one is played very fast, try it with all downstrokes and with alternate picking; use whichever works best for you.

Natural Signs (♮) cancel sharp (♯) or flat (♭) signs, returning the note to its *natural* pitch.

Example 100: The "E" Boogie Pattern, Variation 5

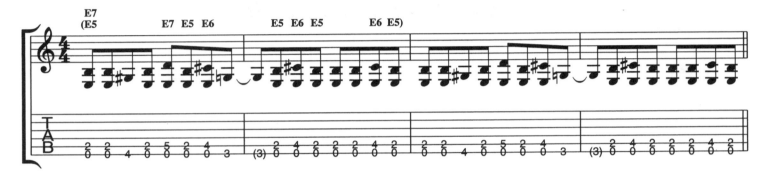

Now transpose the pattern to the root ⑤ A chord.

Example 101: The "A" Boogie Pattern, Variation 5

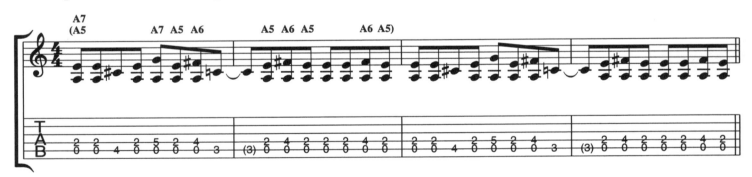

Now transpose it to the root ④ D chord.

Example 102: The "D" Boogie Pattern, Variation 5

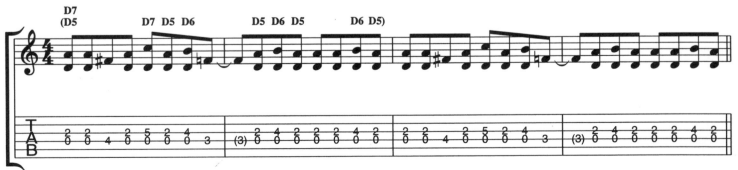

Boogie Pattern, Variation 5

(The "Rock and Roll" Pattern)

Example 103

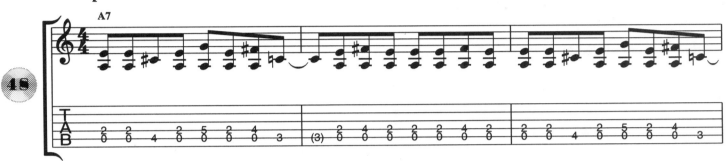

49

The Minor Pentatonic Scale is by far the most common scale used by rock lead guitarists. The notes played by the lead guitarist must fit the chords they are being played over. In many rock tunes, one minor pentatonic scale fits all of the chords. All of the rhythm guitar patterns played so far have been in the key of A. The A minor pentatonic scale would be the best scale choice for developing a lead.

As you already know, the minor pentatonic scale is a five-note scale. The scale construction is: 1 ♭3 4 5 ♭7

A Minor Pentatonic Scale Construction:

A Major Scale:	A	B	C♯	D	E	F♯	G♯	A
	1	2	3	4	5	6	7	8
A Minor Pentatonic:	A		C	D	E		G	A
	1		♭3	4	5		♭7	8

You've already studied the one octave A minor pentatonic scale, now here is the complete first position fingering. This is an extension of the root ⑤ A minor pentatonic fingering studied on page 26. Memorize it. This fingering is one of the most common used by lead guitarists in all styles.

A Minor Pentatonic, Root ⑤

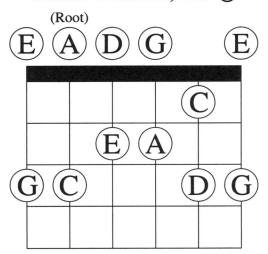

Example 104

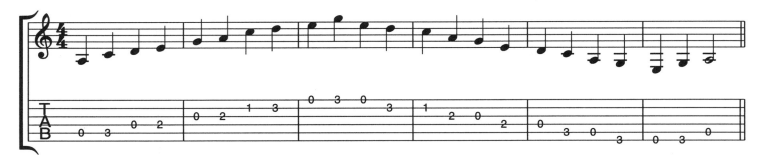

Developing a Lead Guitar Solo: Many beginning lead players start by playing one scale that fits over all the chords—without any regard for the individual chord changes. But in order to play a really good solo you must be very aware of each chord and how the notes you are playing relate to those chords. Listen to Eric Clapton, Stevie Ray Vaughan, Van Halen or Mark Knopfler—every note they play "locks in" to the chord changes.

Each of the upcoming lead riffs is derived from the A minor pentatonic scale, they use the "Target Tone" concept (you may want to review page 36) as a way of focusing the solo on each individual chord change.

Lead Riff 1 is a simple eighth note pattern. It uses every note of the A minor pentatonic scale (in one octave). The riff can be played over every chord with only the target tone (the root of the chord) changing.

Example 105: Lead Riff 1 (with A as the target tone)

Example 106: Lead Riff 1 (with D as the target tone)

Example 107: Lead Riff 1 (with E as the target tone)

Lead Riffs and Patterns

Now play Lead Riff 1 over the 12-bar blues progression. Play all lead riffs with the recording until you've got them mastered, then turn your balance control to the right channel and play the riffs with the rhythm section alone. Once you are comfortable with that, try combining the riffs and playing variations of them.

As you begin to make up your own variations, and spontaneously combine different riffs and licks, you are on your way towards becoming a great lead player.

Lead Riff 1

Example 108

Lead Riff 2 uses the hammer-on technique (review page 52). Like Rhythm Riff 5, this riff begins on a pick-up measure. Once you've mastered Lead Riff 2, learn the two variations: Lead Riffs 2A and 2B.

Example 109: Lead Riff 2

This riff is shown with A as the target tone, the D and E target tones are in parenthesis. First practice the riff resolving to the A target tone, then to the D and E target tones. Notice how the target tone "signals" each new chord change.

Example 110

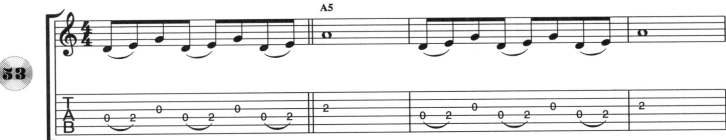

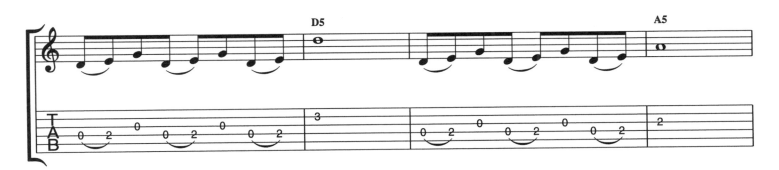

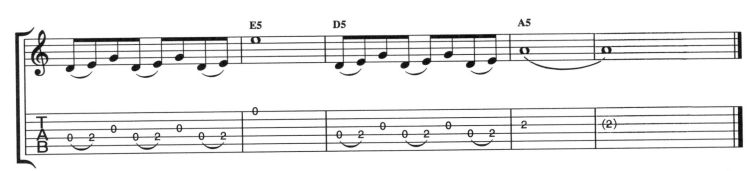

Example 111: Lead Riff 3

Lead Riff 3 uses the **slide technique** (indicated by a slur marking and a diagonal line in between the notes). Play the second string D with your third finger, then slide it up to the second string E (fifth fret). Do not strike the string again with your pick; the second E should be sounded by the force of the finger sliding on to the fret. The next E is played on the open first string. (Again, the riff is shown with A as the target tone, the D and E target tones are in parenthesis.)

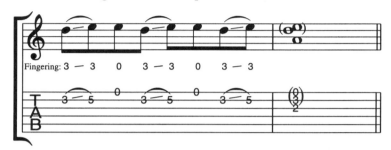

The slide technique is a very important one to develop. Make sure the eighth note rhythm is even. Listen to the recording.

Lead Riff 3

Example 112

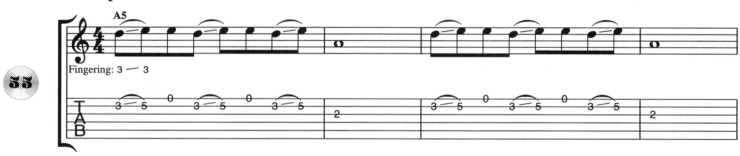

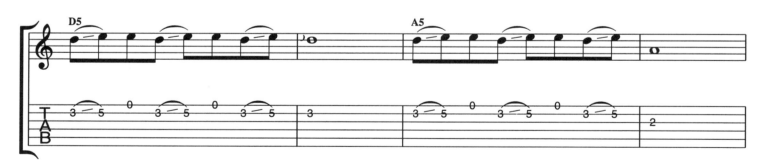

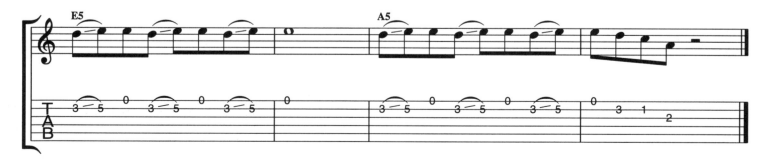

56 Lead Riff 4 is based on a classic lick from *All Your Love* by Otis Rush. This same lick has been used by Eric Clapton, Gary Moore and many others. Note that this lick begins on a pick-up measure.

Example 113: Lead Riff 4

Lead Riff 4

Example 114

57

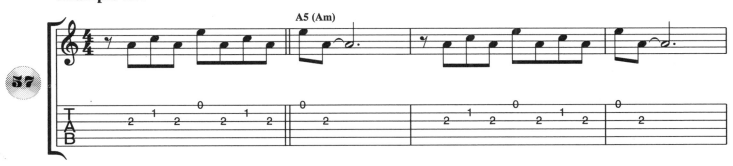

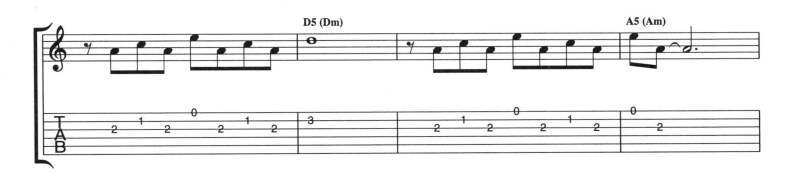

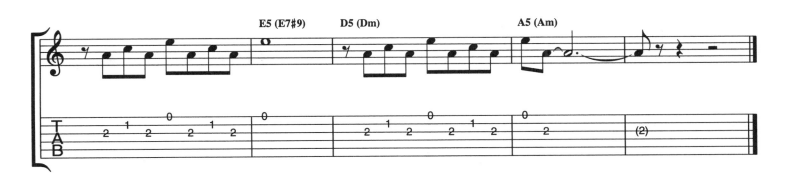

Getting It Together is an example of how each of these riffs can be combined, altered and varied. Keep experimenting—remove the lead guitar from the recording and play along with the rhythm tracks. Each lick, riff, pattern, scale and idea you learn must be practiced until they are second nature and come easily to you.

Getting It Together

Example 115

Lead Riff 1 (one octave lower) - Lead Riff 2 -

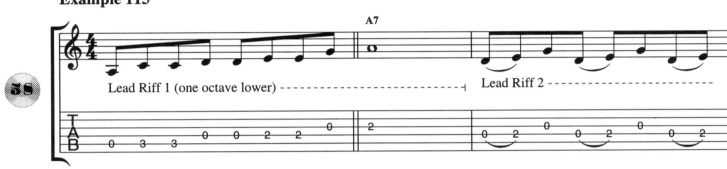

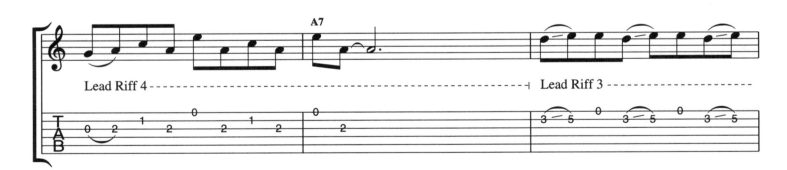

Lead Riff 4 - Lead Riff 3 - - - - - - - - - - - - - - - -

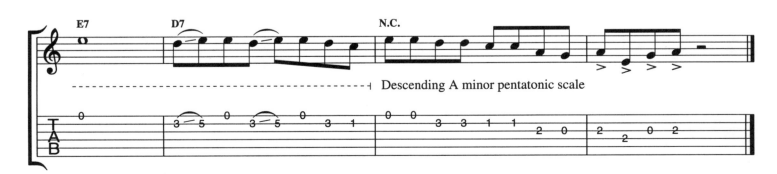

Descending A minor pentatonic scale

Most of the rhythm and lead riff ideas presented in this book are shown here, played over an A chord. Use these two pages as a review and a daily warm-up. Transpose each pattern to D and E and play over a 12-bar blues form in A. The original exercise number is shown for ease of reference. You may want to remove these pages and place them in a separate notebook. By reviewing all of this material daily, these ideas will soon be "at your fingertips." You will then be able to alter and manipulate them to suit your own musical situations.

Example 30: Hard Rock Blues

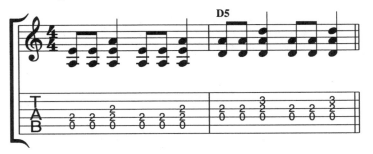

Example 40: Bass Line Pattern 1

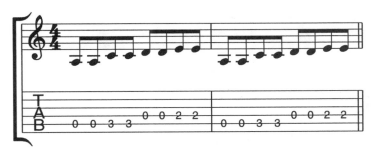

Example 41: Bass Line Pattern 2

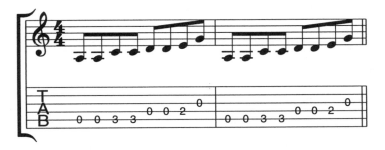

Example 42: Bass Line Pattern 3

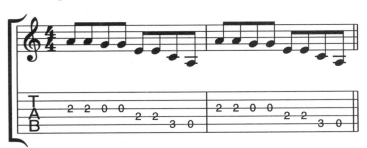

Example 54: Riff 1

Example 58: Riff 2 (Crossroads Riff)

Example 62: Riff 3 (Under Pressure Riff)

Example 66: Riff 4 (Jumpin' Jack Flash Riff)

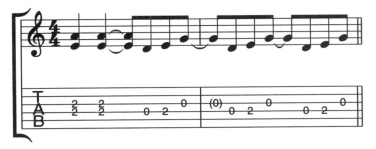

Riff Review

Example 70: Riff 5 (Buddy Guy Riff)

Example 81: Boogie Pattern

Example 85: Boogie Pattern (Variation 1)

Example 91: Boogie Pattern (Variation 2)

Example 95: Boogie Pattern (Variation 3)

Example 99: Boogie Pattern (Variation 4)

Example 103: Boogie Pattern (Variation 5)

Example 108: Lead Riff 1

Example 110: Lead Riff 2

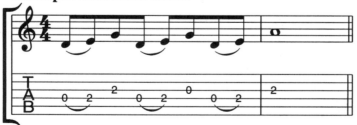

Example 112: Lead Riff 3

Example 114: Lead Riff 4